when the angel of prosperity comes to your house

Prophet Floyd Anthony Barber, Jr.

The Prophetic Society
ALPHARETTA

Copyright © 2015 by Prophet Floyd Anthony Barber, Jr.

All worldwide rights are reserved. No part of this book may be reproduced in any form or by any electronic or mechanical means including information storage and retrieval systems without permission in writing from the publisher except by a reviewer, who may quote brief passages in a review.

The author reserves the moral right to be identified as the author of this work.

Published by:

The Prophetic Society   P.O. Box 206   Alpharetta, GA 30009.

Barber, Floyd Anthony

   When the angel of prosperity comes to your house / Floyd Anthony Barber, Jr.

   1.   Prosperity.   2. Angel lore.   3. Christianity.

For speaking engagements, or to receive prayer for a blessing from the angel of prosperity, contact Prophet Barber @ The Prophetic Society   •   P.O. Box 206   •   Alpharetta, GA 30009.

For worldwide distribution.

Printed and bound in the United States of America.

Unless otherwise noted, all Scripture quotations are taken from the Authorized King James Version of the Bible with Apocrypha. It is historical fact that Jesus and His apostles taught from the Septuagint translation of the Bible (the Greek translation of the Old Testament also known as the Alexandrian Canon) which recognizes the so-called apocryphal books as inspired Scripture. In keeping with their example, the author quotes authoritatively from the so-called apocryphal books as freely as he does from the so-called "Textus Receptus" (also known as the Masoretic Text or Jerusalem Canon).

Second paperback edition.

when

the

angel

of

prosperity

comes

to

your

house

"Beloved, I wish above all things that thou mayest prosper."

-3 John 2

To my beloved Father, Floyd Barber, Sr.

Thank you for your kindness. You are greatly missed.

ABOUT THE AUTHOR

Prophet Floyd Anthony Barber, Jr. was born in New York City. While he was yet young and tender, he and his family relocated to the quaint suburb of Summit, New Jersey. It was there that Providence preserved him until the appointed time of his ministry.

At the age of 19, he received Jesus Christ as his Lord and Savior. Shortly, thereafter, he had an angelic visitation in the night. He then knew that he was called to do a work for the Lord.

Since that time, Prophet Barber has gone on to become an ordained minister. His prophetic ministry flows with balance and accuracy, whereas his teaching ministry is punctuated with depth and clarity, being confirmed by various charisms of the Spirit of God.

Prophet Barber has traveled across the United States ministering in churches, tent meetings, colleges and universities. He has also held associate and senior pastor positions in New Jersey, Missouri, Virginia, California, and Georgia in addition to faculty positions at Ekklesia School of Ministry and the Dr. Dorenza A. Gerrell Institute for Biblical Studies.

In 1993, Prophet Barber studied Tanakh (Hebrew Bible) at the Center for Jewish Life at Princeton University. In the same year his radio program-- The Princetonian Prophet-- was the most popular program on WIMG 1300 in the Greater Trenton area. He was also a featured columnist for Philadelphia's Anointed News Journal, and Newark's Visions newspaper.

In 2004, Prophet Barber relocated to Alpharetta, Georgia where he now resides as the chief executive officer of The Prophetic Society.

ABOUT THE PROPHETIC SOCIETY

The Prophetic Society is a Christ-centered ministry devoted to restoring the ministry of the prophet to its original place of centrality, both in the Church and in the world at large.

The Prophetic Society

Post Office Box 206

Alpharetta, Georgia 30009

An Echo of Eternity

CONTENTS

	About the Author	*vi*
	About The Prophetic Society	*viii*
	Introduction	*ix*
1	**GOD CARES ABOUT YOU**	
	You Are Special to God	1
	God Dotes Over You	2
	A Lifetime of Pleasures	3
	Time To Enjoy!	4
	Change Your Expectancies	5
	The Oil of Prosperity	7
	Nothing Is Impossible	7
	He Satisfies!	9
2	**THE POWER OF MONEY**	
	God on Earth	11
	As Beautiful As Roses	12
	Curse Not The Rich	13
	The Answer To Everything!	14
	Your Right To Be Rich	16
	The Eternal Playwright	16
	Prosperity Now!	18
	It's Your Time	19

3   SACRED MYSTERIES

God Has Secrets	21
The Ages To Come	22
A Prosperity Secret	23
The Prosperity Movement	24
Prosperity Miracles	26
Strange Acts	27

4   BELIEVE HIS PROPHETS

God's Stockbrokers	29
His Proper Gift	30
The Prophet's Reward	30
He Is A Prophet	32
Still In The Pudding	33
The Fullness of Time	34
Victim Souls	35
My Calvary	38
The Power of Forgiveness	42
A Melodious Voice	44
Suffering Affliction	45
The Mystery Revealed	46
Elected To Suffer	48

5   **PROSPERITY COMETH!**

      Slaves of Love   51

      Strength Excelling   52

      Spirits of the Prophets   53

      That Foe Infernal   55

      Savior From Poverty   60

      Cases In Point   62

      Two Paths To Riches   65

      He Blessed Them There   68

      The Moment of Truth   71

INTRODUCTION

"They shall spend their days in prosperity and their years in pleasures."

Job 36:11

Today, no matter where you find yourself in the world, the one thing that people complain about most, on a daily basis, is *money*. Someone once said, *"The lack of money is the root of all evil."* Each day, the truth of this statement is eloquently played out upon the platform of history as record numbers of divorce, starvation, war, disease, crime, and a host of other evils plague our world, all because of a lack of money.

But what if the lack of money were simply an illusion? What if there really were no such thing as lack? Or, better yet, what if there was no lack of sufficient supply of money on earth, but only a lack of *demand* upon the supply of money already available? What if poverty and financial problems simply had to do with a lack of demand upon the supply of money already available? Would that change things for the human populace, as far as quality of life goes? Indeed, it would. Yet noted economists conservatively estimate that there *is* already enough money in the world for all 7.2 billion people to live in peace and prosperity. Moreover, God's Word, the Bible, declares the world to be a place of lavish abundance, saying,

O Lord, how manifold are Thy works! in wisdom hast Thou made them all: the earth is full of thy riches. So *is* this great and wide sea, wherein *are* things creeping innumerable, both small and great beasts.

Psalm 104:24, 25

This proves that lack truly is a mirage. Settle in your heart, once and for all, that there is no such thing as lack. Look out your window and see that you are completely surrounded by abundance.

Those who go without do so only because they have yet to learn the various ways in which to access the immense wealth that is already here, wealth available for the picking at any time. There are natural ways and there are *super*natural ways to draw this abundance to yourself. This book is an ode to the latter.

Enjoy!

CHAPTER 1

GOD CARES ABOUT YOU

"Casting all your care upon Him; for He careth for you."

1 Peter 5:7

You Are Special To God

God cares about you! Yes, in the midst of all the pain and turmoil surrounding you in this topsy-turvy world, Almighty God--the Creator of the Universe--wants you to know that He loves you, and that He cares deeply about you and all the things that are important to you. And this care He has for you is unique in relation to His care for all others.

You are special to God! Just as there are no two snowflakes alike, so too, there is no other person on earth quite like you. Because of this, God wants to have a special relationship with you so that, within the context of this intimate relationship, He can do things for you in a way that He will do for no one else.

God created you to be the fascinatingly complex individual that you are; an individual having special needs and desires that blend together in a very distinct and particular way. And so complex and intricate are your needs and desires that no human being, no matter how well supplied, is quite capable of giving you all that you could ever need or want. Only someone as infinite in wisdom, power, and love as your Heavenly Father can grant you all that you could ever imagine yourself being, doing, and having. That is why, through the oracle of this book, God is going to teach you how to open your life to His prosperity angel so that you can be marvelously blessed and see all of your dreams come true. As it is written in the Scriptures,

And they shall be all taught of God.

John 6:45

God Dotes Over You

Some people think that God doesn't care about them in one way or another. Some even go so far as to think that God actually dislikes them, and that in some way, shape, or form, He is personally responsible for all the mishaps and bad experiences of their lives. So naturally, they blame Him for all their misfortunes. But the truth of the matter is this: *God is a loving, heavenly Father who actually dotes over His children* and it hurts His fatherly heart to know that many of them feel as if He doesn't care about them.

Perhaps, at one time or another, you, too, felt as if God didn't care about you. Maybe you still feel this way. Yet, nothing could be further from the truth because the absolutely greatest thing about life, giving it its ultimate sense of meaning and purpose, is the fact that *God really does care about you!*

Just look around you and see multiple species of birds chirping ever so cheerfully as together they kiss yet another morning's sunrise. Then, turn your attention to the culinary world and let your taste buds leap for joy amidst a myriad of delectable foods bursting with an unlimited variety of tantalizing flavors. While you're at it, take a minute to gaze upward at the parade of cotton white clouds tiptoeing ever so quietly across the backdrop of a powder blue sky. Next, pause in silent reverence, at least long enough to inhale the intoxicating fragrance coming from that nearby garden of exotic tulips encircled with an entourage of silky red roses. And if you'll be still for a moment, you may be able to hear the enchanting sounds of musical quatrains floating across the ethers of the air, nurturing the imagination of all things living. Look behind you and see the neighborhood children splashing playfully in puddles of H_2O as a million little droplets of tender rain join together in quenching the Earth's thirst. Then finally, unwind at eventide as stars innumerable shimmer never so softly like celestial diamonds against the black velvet expanse of our ever evolving universe.

All of these things (and more) testify unanimously to the fact that the Creator really *does* care about you. How so? Because all of these things were created by God for one purpose--to bring you *pleasure!*

A Lifetime of Pleasures

One of the most exhilarating experiences of all is when you come to an understanding that your heavenly Father wants you to have a beautiful life, a fulfilling life, a life filled with peace and happiness, and all the wonderful things that can bring you pleasure! If this were not true, why, then, did the Lord invest so much time in creating you? Moreover, think about all the effort that went into creating the wondrous world in which you now live. What is the reason for God doing all these things? The Bible tells us clearly, saying,

Thou art worthy, O Lord, to receive glory and honor and power: for Thou hast created all things, and for Thy pleasure they are and were created.

Revelation 4:11

Yes, for God's pleasure you are and were created! And if at first this may seem a bit selfish on the part of the Most High, meditate for a moment upon one of the most beautiful truths in all of Scripture:

Let the Lord be magnified, which hath pleasure in the prosperity of His servant."

Psalm 35:27

Clearly, the Father created you for His pleasure. But the way in which He derives this pleasure is not by seeing you suffer in life, nor by seeing you go with unfulfilled hopes and dreams. On the contrary, God gets pleasure by seeing you--His very own child--prosper in life! Why? Because prosperity brings *you* pleasure! Indeed, your ability to experience full and complete pleasure in life is largely determined by how financially prosperous you are. Prosperity is antithetical to poverty. And just as poverty fills life with frustration and misery, so prosperity--its polar opposite--fills life with a great sense of celebration and happiness.

Now you understand why God, like any loving heavenly father, is only pleased to the extent that He sees *you* pleased. And you will only be pleased with the way your life is going when you are financially prosperous enough to be, to do, and to have all you could ever dream of in life, without limit.

No wonder the Bible insists,

If they obey and serve Him, they shall spend their days in prosperity and their years in pleasures.

Job 36:11

Time To Enjoy!

Celebrate the fact that Almighty God wants you--His very own child--to spend each day of your life in *prosperity* and every year that you live upon this lavish earth in *pleasures!* Not pleasure, singular, but pleasures, *plural!* By this can't you see just how much

God truly loves you? He cares about you so dearly that He doesn't want you to enjoy only one kind of pleasure in life. The Lord knows that would be entirely too limiting for you. That is why He wants you to enjoy many kinds of pleasures; literally, *pleasures galore!* These pleasures are the things that nurture your five, God-given senses--your sense of *sight,* your sense of *sound,* your sense of *smell,* your sense of *taste,* and your sense of *touch*--all being titillated by the vast array of amazing things this world has to offer.

Your Father which is in Heaven is a God of abundance and He wants you to enjoy, without limit, all the beautiful things that life can afford. That is why the Bible emphatically declares that the Lord our God is,

> **...the living God, who giveth us richly all things to enjoy.**
>
> 1 Timothy 6:17

All things to enjoy! Does this seem too good to be true? Well, perish the thought because once you come to the place where you understand, *truly* understand, how God feels about you, you will then know beyond any shadow of a doubt that nothing is too good to be true. In this magnificent world of abundance, your heavenly Father wants to pamper you with all the good you could ever desire. As it is written in the Holy Manuscript,

> **Thou openest Thine hand, and satisfiest the desire of every living thing.**
>
> Psalm 145:16

Change Your Expectancies

One of the most exhilarating things God has to say to you in His Word is this:

For I know the thoughts I think toward you, saith the Lord, thoughts of peace, and not of evil, to give you an expected end.

Jeremiah 29:11

Think about that! God only has *peaceful* thoughts about you; *loving* and *kind* thoughts about you, and this same God wants to give you an "expected end."

Simply put, your heavenly Father wants you to know what kind of future you can expect for yourself. Yes, every child of God has an inalienable right to know what his or her future holds. And since you are God's very own child, what exactly does your future hold? The sweet psalmist of Israel wrote,

Surely goodness and mercy shall follow me all the days of my life.

Psalm 23:6

What has been following you throughout the course of your life until now? Has it been sickness? Disease? Money Problems? Frustrating Relationships? Personal setbacks? Some other kind of misfortune? Well, from this day forward I want you to *change your expectancies* because today is a new day for you! Begin now to expect *Goodness* and *Mercy*--those fraternal twins of God's blessings--to follow you for the rest of your life. Why? Because that glorious angel of prosperity is standing on the edge of Paradise waiting for the moment when you will catch the revelation of his reality so he can swoop down and bless you with the riches of God's bounty!

As the prophet of old foretold,

The Lord, before whom I walk, will send His angel with thee, and prosper thy way.

Genesis 24:40

The Oil of Prosperity

Indeed, He whom the ancient scriptures refer to as Jehovah Jireh is about to bellow from the heavens, commanding His angel to fly swiftly with sacred vial in hand in order to come and pour out upon you the mighty *oil of prosperity!*

Stand in awe of the fact that there truly is an "oil of prosperity." What exactly is this mysterious oil, pray tell? Behold, I show you a mystery--the oil of prosperity is a divine concoction mixed eons ago in a far away undisclosed laboratory of sorts (located somewhere within the upper regions of the twelve heavens); a place where only a select group of divinely approved alchemists have their dwelling. And into a consecrated vase this holy oil was poured, then presented with regal pomp and ceremony by Christ Himself to a chosen angel (whose name, incidentally, is secret). Then, on the very day of that grand occasion, God solemnly decreed that upon whomsoever this prosperity oil is poured, that individual will receive the supernatural grace to prosper. Moreover, its most striking feature is that, no matter how often or much the angel pours from this holy vial, the contents thereof can never be fully depleted because, like the fish and loaves of Jesus' day, the oil automatically replenishes itself! And just as this oil has been prospering people for ages untold, this same oil, once poured upon *you* will also cause *you* to prosper beyond your fondest dreams!

Nothing Is Impossible

At this point in your life what exactly is it that you desire to be, to do, to have? Do these things seem just out of your reach? Do they seem impossible to obtain? Do they seem naive or even fairytale-ish? Well, have no fear. Just remember that when a virgin from Nazareth wondered how she could possibly conceive a child without first being intimate with a man, the angel of the Lord said to her,

For with God nothing shall be impossible.

Luke 1:37

No matter how great your desires or how lofty your dreams, your heavenly Father is able to make all these things a living reality for you. And if you still find yourself in the back of your mind somewhere entertaining any doubts about His ability to turn your life into a virtual paradise, the Almighty would ask you this riveting question:

Behold, I am the Lord, the God of all flesh: is there anything too hard for Me?

Jeremiah 32:27

To which, the son of Hilkiah himself would volunteer to respond on your behalf, saying,

Ah Lord God! Behold, Thou hast made the heaven and the earth by Thy great power and stretched out arm, and there is nothing too hard for Thee.

Jeremiah 32:17

He Satisfies!

What do you long for in life? Peace of mind? A healthy body? A new career? A beautiful home? A loving spouse? A happy family? A job promotion? A lucrative business? A dynamic ministry? A college education? A luxury car? A private jet? A yacht? More money? Whatever it may be, revel in the fact that God *satisfies!* Yes, He wants to satisfy the things that you long for in life. As it is written,

He satisfieth the longing soul.

Psalm 107:9

Is this really true? Will God satisfy the longing of your heart? Will He keep His word to you? Can He be trusted to do what He promised? Indeed, He can and He will, for Jehovah would never deceive you. As the book insists,

God is not a man, that He should lie; neither the son of man, that He should repent: hath He said, and shall He not do it? or hath He spoken, and shall He not make it good?

Numbers 23:19

But perhaps you feel unworthy of the Father's blessings, thinking He may grant others *their* heart's desires, but that He's not concerned with doing the same for you. Every person, at one time or another, feels unworthy of God's blessings. In spite of this, however, the Lord still continues to bless them. That is because your heavenly Father loves and adores you just because of who you are-- *His very own child.* And the fact that His only begotten Son, Jesus Christ, gave His life as a sacrifice to God for you makes you worthy of His blessings!

CHAPTER 2

THE POWER OF MONEY

"A feast is made for laughter, and wine maketh merry: but money answereth all things."

Ecclesiastes 10:19

God on Earth

In His infinite goodness and mercy, the Lord of creation has provided the whole of human-kind with all the necessary resources to make life on Earth a virtual paradise of happiness and pleasure. Yet, because each generation produces its share of individuals who, if left unchecked, would maliciously take or withhold these resources from others, long ago a wise and equitable system of exchange was established; a system through which the Creator Himself could work spreading an ethos of fair dealing throughout the Earth. And this medium of exchange through which the Almighty now works is what we affectionately call "money."

Without money, the entire world itself--from its center to its circumference--would eventually implode. That is because, as the Yiddish proverb correctly states,

"The world stands on three things: money, money, and money."

Money is an extraordinarily beautiful concept born long ago in the mind of the Father. In fact, money is a divine idea which God dropped into the imagination of man in order to bring about a sense of justice and equity within the affairs of man. That is why those who criticize and disdain money are divinely disqualified from ever having money in abundance, for to reject money is to reject God because money in a very real sense, is God on earth manifest in the form of paper and ink! That is also why the individual who had the presence of mind to coin the term "Almighty Dollar" deserves our highest accolades.

Yes, when and wherever you see money in circulation, know of a surety that you are witnessing a stark demonstration of the wisdom and power of God!

As Beautiful As Roses

It was the great American essayist of the 19th century, Ralph Waldo Emerson, who wrote,

"Money is, in its effects and laws, as beautiful as roses."

When you thoroughly assess all the progress that the wise and proper use of money has brought, and is presently bringing, to humanity and creation the world over, you, too, will agree that *money is as beautiful as roses.*

Many people speak of money as if it were a dirty thing, as if it were somehow evil. And they attempt to justify their negative attitudes toward money by claiming that the Bible says, *"Money is the root of all evil."* This is a common cliché throughout the Church and society at large, but it is a terrible misquote from Scripture. The scripture they misquote actually says, **"For the love of money is the root of all evil"** (1 Tim. 6:10). Not money, but the *love* of money is the root of all evil. The word "love" here in the original Scriptures means "greed." In other words, having a greedy approach to the acquisition of money is the root of all kinds of evil. Likewise, having a disdain for money is equally as evil. Both attitudes towards money are unacceptable because one can cause you to take or withhold what rightfully belongs to another while the other can lead you to neglect your own personal needs and desires.

If, indeed, money were evil, why do most people spend the majority of their waking hours at their jobs in order to acquire money? Wouldn't that mean working for money is evil? If so, let's all work for free, then, in order to please God. Of course, that would be foolish and impractical seeing we all have bills to pay. Truth be told, lying beneath the surface of every critical word against money is that age-old green monster called "envy."

Curse Not The Rich

Only those who envy the rich spend their time criticizing the rich. In reality, they are not criticizing the rich; they are criticizing *money!* Unconsciously, they are angry at money because, while they find themselves continually struggling to make ends meet, they see money gathering around the rich in abundance. This makes them feel ignored and rejected by money. Nevertheless, (although they would undoubtedly deny this) they wish that they, too, possessed the kind of money they see the rich and famous enjoying.

For this purpose, the richest man in history gave some uncommon advice about this kind of attitude, saying,

Curse not the rich in thy bedchamber: for a bird of the air shall carry the voice, and that which hath wings shall tell the matter.

Ecclesiastes 10:20

This is a tremendous revelation on prosperity, virtually unknown the world over. Here, the sage takes for granted that you already realize that much of your prosperity is going to be funneled by God to you through the hands of wealthy sinners. That is why he previously said,

The wealth of the sinner is laid up for the just.

Proverbs 13:22

But and if you criticize the rich, even in the privacy of your own bedroom, one of the birds of the air that often perch on your window sill will overhear you, then take to the air carrying your words afar. "Bird of the air" is simply a metaphor for *human intuition*. Wherefore, if and when you have the opportunity to meet the rich, they will intuitively feel that you have something against them--and they will avoid you. Of course, all this occurs on the subconscious level because intuition is a thing of the subconscious mind, the same subconscious mind which the Word of God refers to as **"the spirit of man"** (Prov. 18:14).

That is why criticizing the rich in the privacy of your own home is just as real and as damaging as if you criticized them directly to their face. In this you can see the wisdom of the Lord Jesus who encourages you not to criticize but rather to make friends with wealthy sinners (Lk. 16:9) because this will open the way for the angel of prosperity to arrange "divine appointments" that will inaugurate a whole array of opportunities for you to come into great financial prosperity.

Money is as beautiful as roses, a creative concept born in the mind of your heavenly Father. So, it is only appropriate for you to begin taking time each day to inhale the rich aromatic fragrance of money, an olfactory delight sweetly to be urged, to the glory of God!

The Answer To Everything!

Whether the pound, the franc, the marc, the lira, the cedi, the peso, the yen, the rupee, the ruble, or the dollar, when and wherever you see money in circulation--be it given, spent, earned, found, received, printed, invested, manifested, or won--you are witnessing God Himself in operation. Indeed, *Money is the power of God effervescing within the economic sphere of life.*

Money is called "currency" because it was created and intended to flow. That is why the Lord Himself has authorized you to leap into the divine stream of today's Prosperity Movement so that mighty emerald torrents of cold cash can carry you to the very pinnacle of your dreams!

Now take a moment and meditate with me upon one of the most thrilling things the Holy Bible has to say about money:

Money answereth all things

Ecclesiastes 10:19

Yes! *Money answereth all things!* The New American Standard Bible of this passage of Scripture says,

Money is the answer to everything.

Ecclesiastes 10:19

Yes! *Money is the answer to everything!* (Obviously, whoever said money isn't the answer to everything never read this passage in the Bible.)

So, whether "all things" or "everything," the Lord wants you to know that money is the answer to any and every conceivable need or desire you could possibly have. Not the solution, but the *answer.* God is the solution to your problems, but money is the answer to your problems.

And when you pray to the Almighty Solution, He responds by sending the answer!

That is why you must change your attitude towards money, and begin to celebrate and appreciate it for what it is--a beautiful gift from your heavenly Father! And here, in the United States of America, we honor Him for this precious gift the best way we know how--by inscribing upon it, for all nations to see, that most sacred motto: *"In God We Trust."*

Your Right To Be Rich!

What does it mean? In every society throughout this wonderful world in which we live, no matter the language or culture, money has the same identical meaning. Money means freedom, power, influence, beauty, luxury, abundance, security, and refinement. For this purpose, it is written in the oracle of wisdom,

The rich man's wealth is his strong city.

Proverbs 10:15

Indeed, it is the rich man's monetary wealth that gives him all the leverage necessary to make life worth the living in a world where money reigns as king.

The Eternal Playwright

Needs *and* desires! Not either/or, but *both!* This is because when your needs are met you are merely surviving. But when your desires are granted, then you are *thriving!* And God didn't create you merely to survive; He also wants you to *thrive!* In other words, the Lord doesn't want you to be merely sustained in life. He also wants you to be *entertained!* It's a no-brainer that you do not need music, or colors, or flavors, or aromas. It is a fact that you can survive without any of these. So then, what was the Lord's purpose in creating any of these things? To *entertain* you, consummate Host that He is!

Yes, God--the eternal Playwright par excellence--wants you to be happy! And this happiness will become a living reality once you allow Him to open the curtain of abundance, to the end that He may entertain the manifold desires of your heart within the theatre of prosperity. Keep in mind, however, that admission to this theatre is not free. Nothing with the Almighty is free. Indeed, you must *pay* for your ticket. For this purpose, the man after God's own heart said,

I will surely buy it of thee at a price: neither will I offer burnt offerings unto the Lord my God of that which doth cost me nothing. So David bought the threshingfloor and the oxen for fifty shekels of silver.

2 Samuel 24:24

Perish the thought, then, that the best things in life are free. That is the ultimate faux pas. You must *pay* for the best things in life. And the best things in life have always been costly; *very* costly. There was nothing more costly than the redemption of your soul. That is why Christ paid the ultimate price for that redemption--*His life!*

Now you can see why God wants you to have an abundance of money, for, contrary to popular opinion, it is money (and lots of it) that gives you the ability to acquire the things in life that will make you happy.

Never truer words were spoken when Gittel Hudnick quipped, *"Whoever said money can't buy happiness didn't know where to shop."* Selah. And anyone who has an abundance of money to spend as he so chooses, yet still remains unhappy is not because money is unable to buy him happiness; it is simply because he doesn't know what to do with that money!

Prosperity Now!

For this very reason, God wants you to be marvelously prosperous, and He wants you to start enjoying that prosperity right *now!* Not next week or tomorrow, but today, right *now,* at this very moment! That is why, upon realizing it *is* God's perfect will for all of His people to be magnificently prosperous, the psalmist cried out with great jubilation,

O Lord, I beseech thee, send now prosperity!

Psalm 118:25

Indeed, there's no time like the present and there's no day like today! Financial lack is such a dehumanizing thing that your heavenly Father doesn't want you to wait another day on your prosperity. *God is a right now God!* You have waited for prosperity long enough! Since the day you became a child of God by receiving Jesus as your Lord and Savior, you received the divine right to be prosperous. (If you haven't as yet accepted Jesus in this way, then pause for a moment and turn to the last page in this book. With a sincere heart, pray the prayer that you find written there. When you do, Christ Himself will instantly transform you into a child of the Almighty, ushering you into the most beautiful life imaginable. Once you have prayed that prayer, immediately return to this page so I can take you even further into God's mysteries.)

Now, meditate with me upon the absolute wonder of this next glorious truth:

For it is an easy thing in the sight of the Lord on the sudden to make a poor man rich.

Ecclesiasticus 11:21

An easy thing, indeed, as when God took a young man by the name of Joseph, had him released from his prison cell, then exalted him to being the second richest and most powerful person in the world--and He did it all in less than an hour (Gen. 41:1-46)! And since He is no respecter of persons (Rom. 2:11), what the Lord did for Joseph He wants to do for you! Yes, suddenly, without warning, when that mighty angel of prosperity is dispatched from Heaven on your behalf, you will arise from the dungeon of lack and limitation into the ornate palaces of peace and plenty--and no power on earth can stop it!

It's Your Time

The existence of the angel of prosperity remains a mystery to many, but it is no longer a mystery to *you*. And why is that? Jesus said,

Because it is given unto you to know the mysteries of the kingdom of heaven, but to them it is not given.

Matthew 13:11

CHAPTER 3

SACRED MYSTERIES

"Surely the Lord God will do nothing, but He revealeth His secret unto His servants the prophets."

Amos 3:7

God Has Secrets

The Lord has secrets! Some secrets He conceals while other secrets He reveals. Scripture bears witness to the fact, saying,

> The secret things belong unto the Lord our God: but those things which are revealed belong to us and to our children for ever.

Deuteronomy 29:29

When three of His disciples accompanied Him to the top of a high mountain, they witnessed a vision of two of the greatest prophets of Jewish antiquity appearing on Jesus' right side and on His left. Moreover, they heard the majestic voice of the Ancient of Days thunder out of the sky. It was an awe-inspiring, earthshaking event, to say the least. And immediately thereafter, Christ firmly charged them to,

> Tell the vision to no man, until the Son of man be risen again from the dead.

Matthew 17:9

Why did Jesus restrict His disciples from sharing their experience with Him on the holy mount? Why did they have to keep it a secret? It was because Jesus was on a divine mission from the Father, the details of which needed to be kept secret for a time in order for that mission to be accomplished. When a secret is revealed, oftentimes the mere thought about that information can create a "field of interference," thereby hindering the God-intended outcome of that thing, for a secret divulged is a secret indulged.

The Ages To Come

Since the beginning of creation, the Lord has been inclined to whisper profound secrets into the ears of His prophets long before those secrets are ever disclosed to the general public. As the Scripture says,

> **Surely the Lord God will do nothing, but He revealeth his secret unto His servants the prophets.**
>
> Amos 3:7

By virtue of the sanctity of the prophetic office, prophets are granted direct access to many of the Father's secrets. Many of these secrets prophets are permitted to share with others. But many other of these secrets remains for them, and them *alone* to know; secrets the Lord never wants them to share with others, no, not even with other prophets.

The generations of people since the beginning of the common era (i.e., when Christ walked the earth) are the most privileged of all peoples because many divine secrets which were concealed for countless ages have been made known since the coming of the Son of Man (Rom. 16:25-27). This is precisely what the Sacred Record means when it says,

That in the ages to come He might shew the exceeding riches of His grace in His kindness toward us through Christ Jesus.

Ephesians 2:7

Throughout the various ages and epochs of human history, since the resurrection of Jesus Christ, the Creator has revealed the unsearchable riches of His kindness by calling forth His prophets in every generation to unveil to the Church His manifold mysteries, all for the purpose of elevating the people of God to an experience of life grander than that of the angels of Heaven. As it is written,

To the intent that now unto the principalities and powers in heavenly places might be known by the Church the manifold wisdom of God.

Ephesians 3:10

A Prosperity Secret

Because of my particular anointing to be a financial deliverer, the Spirit of the Lord has made me privy to many of His prosperity secrets. And it is my responsibility to unveil to the Church--on a global scale--one of the greatest prosperity secrets of all: *the revelation of the angel of prosperity.* That is why you are reading this book, which is my obedient response to that divine mandate.

The prophet, Abraham, knew who this angel was, for it was he to whom Abraham referred when he said to his servant,

The Lord, before whom I walk, will send His angel with thee, and prosper thy way.

Genesis 24:40

And what exactly is the name of this mysterious angel? Long ago, a devout man by the name of Manoah (i.e. Samson's father) asked the same question. And what was the angel's response?

Why askest thou thus after my name, seeing it is secret?

Judges 13:18

Having been divinely authorized to invoke this angel, I am forbidden to disclose his glorious name lest thou should presume to invoke that wonderful name and thereby incur the disdain of Jehovah. Notwithstanding, be comforted by the fact that the revelation of the angel of prosperity is yet another manifestation of the immensity of your heavenly Father's love for you.

Why this revelation now and not sooner? Because, according to heaven's prophetic timetable, the eternal Godhead (for reasons known only to Them) has deemed this season in the evolution of the cosmos to be the ideal time for the coming forth of a new exhibition of grace, a sudden contraction within the belly of the Church's economic destiny; a stark demonstration of the fiscal might of the everlasting Kingdom of the Almighty!

The Prosperity Movement

The sudden deluge of prosperity literature and media which has been pouring forth since the final decade of the past century is proof positive that we have now entered the age of the "Prosperity Movement." This movement, with all of its wonderful teacher and preachers, is divinely intended to break the back of poverty so that the children of God may joyfully,

...spend their days in prosperity, and their years in pleasures.

Job 36:11

The divinely appointed leaders of this movement have been called "financial deliverers." They are men and women who have been graced with the miraculous ability to propel people into financial and material abundance. Some have the distinct ability to bring forth prosperity through a simple piece of cloth. Others through consecrated olive oil. Some with blessed spring water. Still others through prayer or prophecy. And the countless testimonials of people from all over the world confirm the efficacy of these means and methods. Truly, as the man from Tarsus noted,

God hath chosen the foolish things of the world to confound the wise.

1 Corinthians 1:27

A certain minister has wisely said, "*Never rebel against the instruction of a financial deliverer God sends to you.*" Indeed, there *are* men and women divinely anointed and appointed to be deliverers to those in financial bondage, individuals who, under inspiration of the Holy Ghost, give instructions that, when followed, culminate in miraculous financial breakthrough. Oftentimes, their instructions seem rather ridiculous or overly simplistic to the rational mind. And it is precisely at those times you must determine within yourself to heed the biblical injunction to,

Trust in the Lord with all thine heart; and lean not unto thine own understanding.

Proverbs 3:5

Prosperity Miracles

Because He is omniscient, God sees the world from an entirely different vantage point than the human populace, a point of view that, while appearing at times to be foolish, nevertheless is actually superior to human perception. For this purpose, He said,

For as the heavens are higher than the earth, so are My ways higher than your ways, and My thoughts higher than your thoughts.

Isaiah 55:9

A military leader--through the Spirit--gave a simple instruction to an army of inexperienced soldiers, an instruction that appeared to be incredibly foolish. Yet, because they heeded the instruction, they experienced a *prosperity miracle* (Jos. 6:1-27).

A prophet--through the Spirit--gave a simple instruction to an impoverished woman in the land of Zarephath, an instruction that appeared to be incredibly foolish. Yet, because she heeded the instruction, she experienced a *prosperity miracle* (1 Kgs. 17:8-16).

A prophet--through the Spirit--gave a simple instruction to a woman who, due to the untimely death of her husband, suddenly found herself in a world of debt, an instruction that appeared to be incredibly foolish. Yet, because she heeded the instruction, she experienced a *prosperity miracle* (2 Kgs. 4:1-7).

Sacred Mysteries / 27

The Son of God--through the Spirit--gave a simple instruction to a disciple of His who needed to pay taxes, an instruction that appeared to be incredibly foolish. Yet, because he heeded the instruction, he experienced a *prosperity miracle* (Matt. 17:24-27).

On the flipside, a prophet--through the Spirit--gave a man a simple instruction, an instruction which the man absolutely refused to obey. Eventually, *it cost the man his life* (Acts 21:3, 4 c.f. 2 Tim. 4:6-8). There is no wonder as to why the son of Amoz wrote,

If ye be willing and obedient, ye shall eat the good of the land: but if ye refuse and rebel, ye shall be devoured with the sword: for the mouth of the Lord hath spoken it.

Isaiah 1:19,20

Strange Acts

These few examples provide support for those times when you may feel tempted to disregard the instruction of a financial deliverer. It is important to keep this in mind because, in the next and final chapters, I'm going to talk to you about some cryptic experiences that occurred in my life and ministry, strange occurrences that are all true but that reveal the enigmatic ways in which the Lord works with His servants, the prophets.

Prepare to be dazzled, then, by the sheer beauty of the sacred pearls about to be unveiled to you from the infinite storehouse of the omniconsciousness of God, so that within your life,

He may do His work, His strange work; and bring to pass His act, His strange act.

Isaiah 28:21

Finally, I'm going to give you a simple instruction. If you will believe and heed that instruction, your obedience will unlock God's treasure house of prosperity miracles, ushering you into a strange and exciting new life, all for His glory.

CHAPTER 4

BELIEVE HIS PROPHETS

"Believe in the Lord your God, so shall ye be established; believe His prophets, so shall ye prosper."

2 Chronicles 20:20

God's Stockbrokers

Your relationship with God is sufficient enough for you to be established, which ensures that you will be supplied with the three basic necessities of life, viz., food, clothing, and shelter (Phil. 4:19). But the Lord doesn't want you to stop there. He wants you to move on to the next level and become exceedingly *prosperous* (Job 36:11)! And by divine design, your prosperity is intricately connected to the ministry of the prophet. Why? Because *prophets are the stockbrokers of the Kingdom of God!* This, then, makes prosperity the natural consequence of heeding their instructions. The people of ancient Israel knew this to be fact. As the Scripture says,

...and they prospered through the prophesying of Haggai the prophet and Zechariah the son of Iddo.

Ezra 6:14

Yes, the prophets, Haggai and Zechariah, prophesied God's people into an extraordinary degree of prosperity. In like manner, I prophesy now that, as you take heed to the revelations and instructions that follow, you will enter your golden age of affluence, and great will be your joy and rejoicing in that day!

His Proper Gift

Although all prophets are divinely empowered to prosper the people of God, the ways in which they bring about that prosperity are varied. Some have the ability to prosper you in one area of your life while others can prosper you in another area. Some are divinely gifted to bring about the prosperity of your soul; others the prosperity of the body; still others are gifted to bring forth the prosperity of relationships. And others the prosperity of one's finances (3 John 2). Some are even "multi-anointed" (if I may coin a neologism) having the God-given ability to bring about prosperity in all areas of life. As the Holy Writ teaches,

But every man hath his proper gift of God, one after this manner, and another after that.

1 Corinthians 7:7

Although I have successfully brought about the prosperity of others in various arenas, my primary anointing functions within the domain of finance and material substance, In order to be blessed by a prophet, the Lord would have you know that it is absolutely imperative that you first "receive" that prophet. And I have been empowered by Heaven to invoke the angel of prosperity to bring financial and material blessings into the lives of all those who receive me.

The Prophet's Reward

Once, while expanding the precepts of the Word of God, Christ dropped this profound nugget of wisdom:

He that receiveth a prophet in the name of a prophet shall receive a prophet's reward.

Matthew 10:41

What exactly is the prophet's "reward" referring to? Clearly, it cannot mean to receive the reward *of* a prophet, for God will reward each of us in the Day of Accountability according to our own individual works. For it is written,

...and every man shall receive his own reward according to his own labour.

1 Corinthians 3:8

The prophet's reward Jesus spoke of means to be rewarded *by* the prophet himself. This means that, whenever you receive either the person or the instruction of a prophet, that prophet will, in turn, reward you by using his particular divine gifting to bless you with what you either need or desire at the time.

This is precisely what the prophet, Elisha, did when a rich woman in the land of Shunem, with her husband's consent, had an addition built onto their house so that they could *receive* the prophet into their home whenever he came to do ministerial business within their city. This same woman, being sterile, never had children. So, the prophet decided to "reward" her for her kindness to him by pronouncing a blessing upon her womb--and less than a year later, by the power of that blessing, she gave birth to a bouncing baby boy (2 Kgs. 4:8-17). Indeed, this modern-day, Western society hasn't even begun to realize the full magnitude of what it truly means to be blessed by a prophet of God!

He Is A Prophet

Inscribed in the poetical books of Scripture you will find this verse:

> **Where the word of a king is, there is power.**
>
> Ecclesiastes 8:4

Within the Book of truth, prophets can be seen anointing, appointing, guiding, chiding, and rebuking throughout the dramatic reigns of the Israelite and Judean dynasties. If, then, there is power in the word of a king, how much more power do you suppose there is in the word of a prophet?!

Abimelech, a pious and wise king, at one time found himself in a serious quandary (Gen. 20:1-6). So, God directed him to go to a man named Abraham, saying,

> **...for he is a prophet, and he shall pray for thee.**
>
> Genesis 20:7

No doubt, King Abimelech was polished and eloquent. And the fact that he could get God's attention through his own prayers proves that he had a measure of influence with the high and lofty One who inhabits eternity. Nevertheless, *God still directed him to go to the prophet to receive prayer.* This plainly shows that a prophet, being an ambassador of Heaven, has more influence with God than any earthly politician, no matter how persuasive or articulate that politician may be. As it is written,

> **For greater is he that prophesieth than he that speaketh in a tongue.**

1 Corinthians 14:5

By divine design, the prophetic office is greater than that of any political office. That is why prophets have appointed men to political office, but no politician may appoint a man to the office of prophet. God reserves that right for Himself alone.

For years now, as a prophet, I have been privileged to call out to the heavens on the behalf of many into the ears of one of the seven archangels of God (i.e., the glorious angel of prosperity). This power of grace that I possess is not for my sake, but yours. Neither is this particular honor due to any special qualities of character. Indeed,

For I know that in me (that is, in my flesh,) dwelleth no good thing.

Romans 7:18

This honor is due mostly to the sanctity of the prophetic office in which I stand.

Still In The Pudding

Of course, anyone can claim to possess the "**powers of the world to come**" (Heb. 6:5). So, what--in His love and wisdom--has your heavenly Father done to protect you from embracing a counterfeit? He has already instructed you about this in the Sacred Pages, declaring,

Whoso boasteth himself of a false gift is like clouds and wind without rain.

Proverbs 25:14

It is as abnormal for a person to possess a divine gifting that produces no results as it is for dark ominous clouds and strong gusts of wind to produce no rain. To claim to have a gift while producing no tangible results is proof positive that the one making the claim possesses no such gifting.

Here is the beauty of common sense: if a man claims to be a pastor yet has no congregation of parishioners, is he truly a pastor? If a man claims to be a surgeon yet has never performed any surgeries, is he truly a surgeon? Beyond the shadow of any doubt, the proverbial proof is still in the pudding. It is necessary that you know this, for the time will come, and now is, when many charlatans will arise claiming to have certain miraculous abilities from God. Some will even have the temerity to claim power over the angel of prosperity while producing no tangible results. The Nazarene Himself cautioned you about such things, forecasting,

And many false prophets shall rise, and shall deceive many.

Matthew 24:11

The presence of the false always affirms the existence of the true, and if the one is truly a prophet, tangible results will confirm the validity of his claims. Moreover, besides spiritual gifts, there are other things which separate the true prophet from the counterfeit. Once you know these things, you then will have found the surest path to true and lasting prosperity.

The Fullness of Time

In order to qualify as a prophet of the living God, it is necessary that one first be born in the "fullness of time." When speaking about the birth of Jesus, Scripture says,

But when the fullness of the time was come, God sent forth His Son, made of a woman, made under the law, to redeem them that are under the law, that we might receive the adoption of sons.

Galatians 4:4, 5

What does this mean by Christ being born in the "fullness of the time"? It is a revelation of the fact that He was born for a specific purpose according to a prophetic time-table predetermined by His Father from the foundation of the world (Gen. 3:15). In like manner, every prophet is born with a divine purpose, and at a time that is ideal to that particular purpose. And since each prophet's purpose is bound to Heaven's calendar, no prophet--no matter how anointed--can counterfeit another's purpose, for each prophet's purpose is unique.

Now what does all this have to do with your prosperity? Everything, for by the determinate counsel and foreknowledge of the Father, my specific purpose for being born at this juncture in history, during *your* lifetime, is so that I may pray for your prosperity.

Victim Souls

Notwithstanding, being born at a certain time period is not always enough, for those endowed with special graces from on high oftentimes must pay a price for those gifts, a heavy price indeed--*suffering!*

Some people suffer because of ignorance, theirs or someone else's. Others suffer because of foolishness, theirs or someone else's. And some suffer because of maliciousness, theirs or someone else's. Yet, in every generation there are those who, because of a divine purpose, suffer for the benefit of others. These individuals have come to be known throughout Christendom as *victim souls.* Such people, like Christ the Lord, have been chosen of the Father to suffer vicariously on the behalf of others. Since God foresees within these people the fortitude to endure extreme sufferings without caving in to the pressure, He selects them to be His victim souls. The divine purpose of their suffering is to bring about other people's glory, for in the economy of God suffering *is* the price of glory. The apostle to the Gentiles--a victim soul--wrote about this very thing, saying,

Therefore I endure all things for the elect's sakes, that they also may obtain the salvation which is in Christ Jesus with eternal glory.

2 Timothy 2:10

Paul endured incredible sufferings among which was his being imprisoned for the better part of his adult life **"for the *elect's* sakes,"** that is, for the express benefit of the people of God so they would **"obtain the *salvation* which is in Christ Jesus."** Indeed, the stripping of his personal freedom through the years of unjust incarceration, along with tribulations too numerous to mention (2 Cor. 11:23-28), resulted in the salvation of many.

The evangelist, Raymond T. Richey, was also a victim soul. As a child he suffered incredible illness within his body. Yet, when he became a young adult, he was divinely graced with the ability to pray for the healing miracles of multitudes. The destruction of his personal health during childhood later translated into the healing of hundreds of thousands of people.

Throughout history, victim souls make up a very small minority of the Christian populace. No one knows whether he/she has been divinely chosen to be a victim soul until they begin experiencing their divinely permitted "season of victimization." And many times they will not even know until some time *after* that season is complete.

God is not the cause of this victimization; Satan is. And a victim soul is one who is divinely elected, at some point in life, to vicariously take on the afflictions the devil intended for others. It is when the few are chosen to suffer for the many; the minority for the majority; the classes for the masses; the seeds for the fruit. Some call this the "mystery of identification" because, in the victim soul's own life and experiences, he/she identifies with the sufferings satanically intended for others. It is when, through their sufferings, others are spared from having to experience these afflictions themselves.

Undoubtedly, the Man from Galilee will forever remain the *ne plus ultra* of all victim souls, having been crucified for the iniquities of all humankind. Our heavenly Father actually took great delight in witnessing His only begotten Son suffer on the cross. Not because He's some sort of cosmic masochist, but rather because, through the suffering of Jesus, many would be spared from the torments of eternal damnation. The prince of prophets commented upon this very thing when he wrote,

Yet it pleased the Lord to bruise Him; He hath put Him to grief.

Isaiah 53:10

Likewise, God rejoices in seeing the sufferings of that handful of people whom He has chosen to be victim souls because, through the incredible sufferings of these few, many will be spared from countless miseries they otherwise would have suffered throughout the course of their lives. That is why Christ celebrated His experience at Calvary, for He knew the joy--both His and that of others--that would come about as a consequence of His vicarious sufferings. For the Scripture says that Jesus,

> **... for the joy that was set before Him endured the cross, despising the shame, and is set down at the right hand of the throne of God.**
>
> Hebrews 12:2

That is also why Paul could celebrate his own vicarious sufferings for the same reasons as Jesus. As he wrote,

> **...who now rejoice in my sufferings for you, and fill up that which is behind of the afflictions of Christ in my flesh for His Body's sake.**
>
> Colossians 1:25

My Calvary

What does the revelation of "victim souls" have to do with your prosperity? Everything, because although I was raised for the greater part of my childhood in one of the most upscale suburbs of North America, having affluent friends, and being educated in an exceptional school system. I personally grew up in extreme poverty. The combined income level of my household should have afforded me a prosperous or, at the very least, a comfortable upbringing. Nevertheless, although the personal needs and extravagances of my mother and stepfather were attended to, I suffered many painful years of abuse and neglect at their hands.

Bouncing from house to house (due to being malnourished at home) incessantly begging "friends" for food until I eventually became the butt of jokes and wisecracks at school; having a maximum of two to three pair of torn or shredded underwear at a time (often hand-me-downs from my next oldest brother); pleading with the janitor at my local church to save me any leftover clothes from the church's periodic rummage sales; seeing the church's choir director feel so sorry for me that she would often bring me a bowl of soup or a sandwich to our weekly choir rehearsals — these were only a fraction of humiliating (albeit, preventable) experiences I endured. Most of my clothes I had to hand wash in the bathtub since I was restricted from using our washing machine. And if I asked for money to go to the Laundromat, or left my clothes to soak in the tub a minute too long, my mother or stepfather would reprimand me almost to the point of terror. So great was the fear that I would go weeks at a time without washing the few clothes I had because it would literally take me that long to muster up the courage to put them in the tub again. As a consequence, wearing soiled clothes became an ordinary part of my childhood. Whenever I could afford it, I would attempt to cover up the odor by smearing my clothing with cheap cologne I would purchase at the local five-and-dime store. Obviously, this was ineffective because I distinctly remember the time when my clothes were so soiled that, at a church gathering for the youth, our church's youth pastor "jokingly" said to the crowd, *"For some reason, Floyd always smells like kitty litter."* On that note, all the kids--preteens and adolescents--exploded into laughter. Deeply wounded, I went away from that experience wondering how that a minister, of all people, could be that cruel and insensitive. And from that day forward I stopped going to that church (or any church) altogether. Neither did a single person from that gathering ever come to see about my wellbeing. In the meanwhile, the abuse and neglect at home continued to escalate.

Finally, by the age of thirteen (a year later) I had had enough. So, I went to my guidance counselor at school and told her, along with two other school officials, the entire plight of my childhood abuse. I told them about all the degradation, the humiliation, and the beatings I suffered at home in quiet desperation. (I would have gone sooner, but it took some time to build up the courage being that my stepfather--an ex-convict--often exploded in sudden frenzies, kicking over tables and ripping doors off of hinges while brandishing a straight razor, threatening to cut my throat; all this before I was even a teenager.) Needless to say, the school officials were shocked and appalled by the things I divulged, so they immediately contacted the Division of Youth & Family Services (DYFS) to handle the situation. Rather unwisely, DYFS notified my mother and stepfather in advance that they would be coming by to investigate the matter. Of course, this gave them (two incredibly shrewd people) ample opportunity to practice putting on airs.

On the appointed day, the people from DYFS arrived to an uncommonly immaculate apartment. (All a front for the occasion.) I had assumed that during the meeting I would be afforded the opportunity to tell the people of DYFS the exact things I suffered at the hands of my parents. Yet, to my utter dismay, I was not permitted to sit in the meeting. Instead, I was asked to remain in my bedroom with the door closed as if they somehow forgot that *I* was the reason for the meeting in the first place! While eavesdropping at the door I caught bits and pieces of my mother and stepfather lying to the DYFS officials, claiming that my accusations of their abuse were all fabricated. They insisted I had not psychologically adjusted, as yet, to the loss of my biological father (who had passed away seven years prior), and that this was the impetus behind my accusations of their abuse. Naturally, I was shocked beyond measure, but took hope assuming that after they were done speaking with my parents, DYFS would then call me out into the living room to hear *my* side of the story. Such was not the case because my mother--silver-tongued to a fault--was so convincing in covering up her and my stepfather's shenanigans that, in less than an hour's time, the people of DYFS simply gathered their things and left. Stunned, I dashed to my bedroom window to see them leave me in my predicament without so much as asking to speak with me! It was an unbelievably surreal, Twilight Zone-like experience as I watched the very organization established for the purpose of rescuing children like myself enter their cars and drive away, never to be heard from again.

Dazed by the impact of what had just transpired, I remember gazing into the sky in a trance-like stupor, completely fixated by the thought of how God could allow something like this to happen to me. When, suddenly, I found myself gripped by an overwhelming sense of dread, knowing that as a form of retribution for having DYFS notified about their abusive ways, my mother and stepfather would only intensify the abuse--and intensify it they did! As soon as I turned to walk away from the window, my stepfather angrily rushed into my bedroom, yelling and cussing me with the usual expletives, while behind him stood my mother glaring at me with that bone-chilling scowl I had become so accustomed to seeing. I recall how my head swooned as I stood there trembling from the memory of all the abuse I had been through up until that point, and from the thought of all the horrors I was bound to face in the years to come.

Some time later (due to my stepfather's gambling habits) we were forcibly "downsized" to what was called a railroad apartment. In another few months, we were downsized again to a studio apartment. And for the next five years I suffered an enormous amount of verbal and physical abuse. I was forced to make the kitchen my bedroom, sleeping between the kitchen sink and the kitchen table on a flimsy aluminum foldout cot (which caused me years of indescribable back pain). I had no dresser to put my clothes, my schoolbooks, nor anything else in. Moreover, I was practically forbidden to eat my parent's food, except during those rare times when they were in "good spirits," allowing me to eat a few of their eggs or a can of their Campbell's pork-and-beans. If in an exceptionally good mood from winning money at the horse races, they would announce their arrival home in the middle of the night by smacking me in the head with a bag containing a hamburger or two from the local Burger Express. Compounding the humiliation was the fact that I even had to ask permission whenever I wanted a glass of tap water. I cried so hard and so frequently due to the abuse that my skin eventually formed two unsightly scar lines down both sides of my face which took years to finally heal. Fortunately, I secured a part-time, after school job at a local business that specialized in supplying parts for musical instruments. And with that $27 per week I was able to start buying myself a little food to eat. As far as my education was concerned, I was considered an exceptionally bright student, designated with a near genius I.Q., but my grades suffered terribly because of the years of emotional duress I experienced at home. Due to extreme sleep deprivation caused by my stepfather repeatedly waking me up on school nights, then shouting at me until the wee hours of the morning about the various ways in which he could cut my throat, I was forced to repeat the 7th grade.

From the time my mother unexpectedly barged into my 3rd grade classroom early one Monday morning, then proceeded to flog me with a leather belt in the presence of my teacher and classmates, until the time when at the age of twenty-six I was contacted by the Social Security office who notified me that, for eleven consecutive years, my mother had received monthly financial assistance from the government due to the death of my biological father, monies which she never told me of, monies which were supposed to be used for *my* well-being while growing up, monies of which not even a small portion, no, not even so much as a dime was put aside for my college education; and all the other incidents of unthinkable humiliation I suffered at her and my stepfather's hands--this, my friend, was my Calvary.

The Power of Forgiveness

It is written in the holy book of Psalms,

Weeping may endure for a night, but joy cometh in the morning.

Psalm 30:5

As a victim of severe child abuse, I wept many a night over many years. Yet, eventually my morning joy came because in the Spring of 1985 I had a life-changing encounter with Jesus Christ! And seven days later I received the gift of the Holy Spirit, a gift which God promised to give all those who simply ask Him (Lk. 11:13; Acts 2:38, 39). I became so euphoric due to an infusion of supernatural joy that all the emotional pain of my childhood experiences instantly vanished. I then began to devour every book I could get my hands on that had to do with Christianity. Eventually, I came across the Bible's teaching about the necessity of forgiving those who mistreat us (Matt. 5:43-48; Mk. 11:25). And because of my newfound relationship with Jesus, I was able to forgive my mother and stepfather for the abuse I suffered at their hands. Notwithstanding, they didn't change their ways because, although the physical abuse stopped (due to the fact I wasn't a little child anymore), their verbal abuse continued. But, by the grace of God, the power of forgiveness made me practically impervious to their remarks (Ps. 119:165). *Unforgiveness is the most destructive force in the universe,* being more powerful than any weapon of mass destruction. That is why you must, for your own sake, find it within yourself to forgive all those who have ever harmed or taken advantage of you in any way, no matter how great the atrocity may have been. If you cannot find the strength to do so, sincerely ask God to give you the strength to forgive, and He will. Understand that forgiveness does not mean putting yourself in a position where abusive people can continue to hurt you. That would be foolishness, not forgiveness. Neither does it mean that people should not be held accountable for their actions, for how then could there be any true expression of justice in the world? Forgiveness simply means a prayerful renunciation of all bitterness and resentment towards those who have wronged you in any way. This is why Jesus taught,

And when ye stand praying, forgive, if ye have ought against any: that your Father also which is in heaven may forgive you your trespasses.

Mark 11:25

What does all of this teaching about abuse and forgiveness have to do with your prosperity? Everything, because the greatest miracles of our lives begin happening when we start practicing the power of forgiveness. I learned this powerful lesson while still a teenager when into that maelstrom of poverty and child abuse--there in the quaint ambiance of Summit, New Jersey--came a heavenly visitor.

A Melodious Voice

In the Spring of 1985, almost two months after I became born again, I heard a melodious, flute-like voice call out to me in the middle of the night, saying, *"Floyd."* At first I thought I was dreaming. But, as I began to doze off, the voice then called out a second time, *"Floyd."* At that moment I perked up, but still though the voice was something I heard in a dream. So, you can only imagine how shocked I was, now that I was wide awake, to hear that same voice call out to me a third time, *"Floyd."* I bolted upright in my bed, astonished beyond description at what I just heard. I felt like the men who traveled with Paul on the road that led to the city of Damascus when Christ suddenly appeared to them in the upper sky. Of this experience, the apostle said,

And they that were with me saw indeed the light, and were afraid; but they heard not the voice of Him that spake with me.

Acts 22:9

My experience was the flipside of that same coin in that I heard the voice of him that spoke to me, but I saw no light, nor any person, yet I knew the voice came from the right side of the foot of my bed because I felt a holy presence emanating from that very spot. Needless to say, I was ecstatic! Struck by the absolute awesomeness of this experience, I began to weep and rejoice almost to the point of hysterics. I tried hard to keep as calm as possible because I could hear my mother and stepfather awake in their room watching television. Not only that, but since the kitchen was my bedroom, I was afraid that --out of sheer excitement over my experience--I might start flailing my arms and inadvertently smack my elbow on one of the legs of the kitchen table.

Then, while crying and quietly praising God, the kitchen suddenly became permeated with a soft heavenly peace. I can fully appreciate the life of Teresa of Avila because, at that precise moment, I, too, went into complete ecstasy. It was hard to believe that this was actually happening to *me,* but it was! (I was to find out later that the prophet, Daniel, was also a teenager, being about the same age I was at the time when he had his first visitation from one of God's holy angels.) No words could ever describe how elated I was by that heavenly encounter.

Suffering Affliction

I went away from that experience with a new zeal for God. But I kept the experience to myself, adopting the posture of that righteous virgin who, after a visitation from the angel, Gabriel, the Scripture says,

> **Mary kept all these things, and pondered them in her heart.**
>
> Luke 2:19

Although I didn't know the Bible very well at the time, I had enough sense to keep the fact of my divine visitation to myself. Actually, I kept these things to myself for fear that someone would think I was either losing my mind or making the whole thing up. So, for the next ten years I never breathed a word of it to anyone, not even to my best friend, although he, too, was a Christian.

Even though no human being knew of the supernatural experience I had that unforgettable night, I knew Satan and his demonic thralls had to have known because, from that night forward, I began to experience a deluge of persecution that made the abuse of my childhood seem like a walk in the park! An eyewitness to the incredible trials which I suffered told me I was the most persecuted Christian he had ever seen in his life. From reading the Scriptures, I knew that persecution was the lot of any true prophet, but even I began to feel that there was something extraordinarily peculiar about the nature and intensity of the persecutions which befell me. Later, I was to discover that there was indeed something unique about my trials and tribulations. For many years it was all a mystery to me, but every now and then I would be granted yet another piece of the puzzle concerning my destiny.

The Mystery Revealed

Believe His Prophets / 47

Who exactly was the heavenly visitor who came to my residence just two months after I embraced the Gospel of Him that died and rose again? His visit with me that night caused a major shift in my spiritual life, whereafter I had the power to heal and even discern the thoughts of people's hearts. I had always assumed that it was Jesus Himself. However, many years after, at a season deemed appropriate by Providence, the Holy Ghost revealed to me that it was actually my divinely appointed partner in ministry--the *angel of prosperity*. Up until that point in time I had never even heard of any such thing as an angel of prosperity. I knew of guardian angels, warrior angels, messenger angels, and even worshipping angels, but not of any so-called *prosperity angel*. The Spirit of God then directed my attention to the holy book of beginnings, which reads,

The Lord, before whom I walk, will send His angel with thee, and prosper thy way.

Genesis 24:40

There it was in plain black and white--an *angel of prosperity!* I was astounded. It was then that I remembered how that the Lord had spoken to me in early 1995 saying He was going to transform me into a "money mystic." So, naturally, I thought to myself, *"Could this Scripture concerning the angel of prosperity and my becoming a money mystic somehow be connected?"* I was soon to find out because as I began testing the waters, so to speak, by praying for people with financial needs or trapped on financial predicaments, they would soon contact me with testimonials about the answers to my prayers, testimonials so amazing that they literally startled me.

What was a mystery to me for so long no longer remained a mystery because the Spirit of the Lord explained to me how the amazing monetary miracles which were happening for people in answer to my prayers was because of the angel of prosperity, an angel divinely commissioned to bring answers to my prayers. At that moment a holy awe washed over me as I stood there thinking that I, of all people had been graced with such an honor. Yet for the next few years, I couldn't help wondering why I had been granted this particular grace.

Elected To Suffer

Eventually, when the Father decided I was spiritually mature enough to receive a full disclosure of my divine purpose in life, the Holy Ghost called me aside into the Scriptures and walked me through the revelation about victim souls. He then explained how the deprivation of my childhood had to do with my being divinely chosen to be a victim soul for the people of God. Finally, it all made sense.

From an earthly standpoint my years of growing up in abject poverty made no sense whatsoever because I lived in an upscale community with a mother who was a medical professional and a stepfather who, although a blue collar worker, their combined salaries were more than enough to provide a comfortable lifestyle, a lifestyle which they often enjoyed for themselves while begrudgingly piecemealing me with hardly the bare necessities of life. And it was precisely because of the affluence of my surroundings that I felt the pain of my poverty all the more accutely.

From a heavenly standpoint, however, the severity of my childhood experience made perfectly good sense. God was not the cause of my poverty. Satan was. And my mother and stepfather were simply willing and yielded instruments of the devil. Of course, they will one day be required to give an account for yielding to the dictates of Satan because, in that they had free will, they had the ability to choose to do the right thing by me. But since by His

Believe His Prophets / 49

foreknowledge, He knew in advance that my parents would abuse and deprive me the way they did, the Lord decided beforehand to bring something redemptive out of my abusive childhood. This He did by ordaining me, while still in my mother's womb, to be a *victim soul*. Divine juxtaposition, indeed! No wonder He stipulated in the Word of His grace,

I am God, and there is none like Me, declaring the end from the beginning, and from ancient times the things that are not yet done, saying, My counsel shall stand, and I will do all My pleasure.

Isaiah 46:9, 10

My poverty in the midst of incredible affluence was indeed an anomaly. But it all turned out for the good because I was nominated by God to suffer those things **"for the elect's sake"** (2 Tim. 2:10). In the mind of the Father I was monetarily plundered and neglected so that--through my vicarious suffering--you would never have to suffer financially. And because of my perseverance through that experience and my subsequent confirmation into the office of prophet, I am duly authorized by the Almighty to invoke the angel of prosperity to bring you into what Jesus Christ endearingly referred to as the *abundant life* (Jn. 10:10).

CHAPTER 5

PROSPERITY COMETH!

"Thus they did day by day, and gathered money in abundance."

2 Chronicles 24:11

Slaves of Love

What exactly are angels? They are the bond slaves of God, created for no other purpose but the doing of the bidding of the Lord. Please do not cringe at the word "slaves" for among the heavenly host there can no angel be found decrying their plight, the reason being there is no abusive element to their slavery whatsoever. Their bondage to God is in all actuality a bondage to *love,* for God Himself *is* love. As it is written,

God is love.

1 John 4:8

It was the holy bishop, Fulton Sheen, who once said, *"If you could only love enough you would be the most powerful person in the world."* Amen.

And no one understands the truth of that statement more than the Lord's angels, for--having sipped softly (for ages untold) of the sweet nectar of the Father's benevolence--angels know by experience that there is no greater power than the power of love.

God is love! This, then, makes His angels the *slaves of love.* It is love that binds them to their Almighty Master. And it is that same love which drives these hallowed angels to be intimately involved in the epic drama of human history. Yes, angels are deeply concerned about the daily challenges you have to face, challenges often imposed upon us by the wicked forces of darkness. For the Scriptures affirm,

> **...which things the angels desire to look into.**
>
> 1 Peter 1:12

Strength Excelling

Child of grace, celebrate the fact that angels--the eternal slaves of your loving heavenly Father--are intensely devoted to aiding you in your fight against the malevolence of the devil. *"But,"* you say, *"are these angels really strong enough to defeat the Adversary of my soul?"* I answer with a resounding *"Yes!"*, for it was not in vain that the son of Jesse cried out to the heavenly host,

> **Bless the Lord, ye His angels, that excel in strength, that do His commandments, hearkening unto the voice of His Word!**
>
> Psalm 103:20

God's angels excel in strength! Just as they were strong enough to expel Lucifer and his minions from the heavenly realms long ago (Lk. 10:18 c.f. Rev. 12:7-9), they possess that same strength even now. And because they genuinely care about you, these mighty celestial beings are more than willing and ready to drive the devil out of your life!

Remember that only a minority of angels sided with Lucifer in his failed coup against the sovereign Lord, but it was the remaining majority that defeated these renegade angels at the frontier between Heaven and Earth (Isa. 14:12-15 c.f. Rev. 12:3, 4). So, be encouraged by the fact that the same majority is on our side! As the prophet exhorted,

Fear not: for they that be with us are more than they that be with them.

2 Kings 6:16

Spirits of the Prophets

It is written in the Holy Scriptures,

And the spirits of the prophets are subject to the prophets.

1 Corinthians 14:32

What exactly are the "spirits" of the prophets? They are none other than the Lord's holy angels! For the Word of truth says that God,

...maketh His angels spirits.

Psalm 104:4

Angels are spirits! They are invisible to the naked eye, but just as real as the sun, moon, and stars. And a number of these angels

Scripture calls the "spirits of the prophets" because many of these very same spirits are divinely commissioned to work with the ministries of God's seers.

Every prophet has at least one angelic spirit who has been assigned by God to work with that prophet's ministry. Some prophets (based upon the breadth and scope of their calling) even have an entourage of angels working with them to bring about the express purposes of God in the earth. That is why all throughout the pages of the Book of the Lord you read about multitudes of angels appearing to, and on the behalf of, God's prophets more than any other people.

On a number of occasions a messenger angel worked with the prophet, Daniel, bringing him apocalyptic revelations directly from the Throne of glory. Why? Because that spirit was subject to the prophet's ministry.

Moreover, on many occasions the healing angel worked with the prophet, William Branham, assisting him with healing infirmities no matter where in the world he could be found praying for the sick. Why? Because that spirit was subject to that prophet's ministry.

And for many years now, the prosperity angel (whose name is secret) has worked with me in unleashing prosperity miracles for all those that I pray for. Why? Because that spirit--by the determinate counsel and foreknowledge of the Father--is subject to my ministry.

That is why the ministry of the prophet is so vital to the divine scheme of things because no one can give directives to an angel simply because they choose to do so, no matter how sincere or great their faith in God may be. Indeed, *one must be duly authorized to invoke these angels!* And it is the prophets who have received this authority from the Creator Himself. Happily, this acts as a spiritual safeguard to protect people from various impostors who--being vain and opportunistic--often attempt to mimic the ministries of the Lord's seers. For, as we see in the case of the prophet, Elijah, if one

Prosperity Cometh / 55

is truly a prophet, graced with miraculous abilities, the Lord will confirm the ministry of that prophet by unmistakable demonstrations of His power (1 Kgs. 18:1-40; Ecclus. 48:1-11).

Some time ago a pastor, upon hearing about my influence over the angel of prosperity, presumed to invoke he whose name is secret, attempting to persuade this devout spirit to bring a certain amount of money to him in order to cover a pressing financial need. Of course, nothing happened. Over a period of weeks he attempted, over and again, to invoke the angel of prosperity, all to no avail. What this cleric failed to realize is that God is absolute and does not vulgarly bend His will to the whims of any, no, not even to His ministers. That is why the Lord admonishes His people, saying,

Let every man abide in the same calling wherein he was called.

1 Corinthians 7:20

It is a mark of wisdom and true humility for an individual to continue doing whatever it is that God has called him/her to do, and not to presume to usurp another's anointing. If God has indeed endowed a person with the same type of anointing as another, He will make it known to that person. Moreover, the fruit of that individual's ministry will bear witness to that fact for all to see. As it is written,

A man's gift maketh room for him, and bringeth him before great men.

Proverbs 18:16

That Foe Infernal

56 / When The Angel of Prosperity Comes To Your House

What startled Martin Luther (the 15th century monk who single-handedly revolutionized a near dead Church virtually overnight) to such an extent that, if you were to visit his home--a home that is standing to this very day in Wittenberg, Germany--there you would find a large ink blot on the wall of his study, the consequences of his having hurled an ink bottle through the air? Or, what moved Dr. Lester Sumerall, one of the saintliest ministers of the 20th century, to cringe in fear one evening shortly after he entered his hotel room during a week of evangelistic crusades in Java, Indonesia? Let me tell you: it was that same individual who came upon me unawares on that dreadful morn of May 2, 2001.

Just two weeks before, I finally found the courage to publicly speak, for the first time, about my visitation from the prosperity angel back in the Spring of 1985, and to tell about my divine authorization to direct the activities of this angel. Up until that time I had only shared my experience with people on a one-to-one basis, or at times in small group settings. But through time and prayer, I eventually overcame my apprehension about the repercussions that would undoubtedly come from sharing such an astounding revelation, viz., the inevitable backlash that often comes due to the ignorance, envy, or unbelief of others.

So I stepped into the pulpit of a church in northern New Jersey that Sunday afternoon in 2001 and for the first time taught publicly about the existence of an "angel of prosperity," informing the congregation that God charged His angel to be subject to my ministry. The people rejoiced. And from that moment onward, starting with a woman from an inner-city slum, people began experiencing astounding prosperity miracles in response to my prayers.

Then, exactly a week later, an unusually wicked demon appeared to me in my dreams. I distinctly remember how that the precise moment our eyes met, the demon, in an unnervingly ghoulish tone, said to me, *"You!"* Although it was a dream, I could somehow feel that one word cut to the core of my soul striking me with a sensation of fear I had never before experienced. So great was the fear that it took me no less than three days to even begin recuperating from the emotional shock of it all. But no sooner than I began to get over the sheer trauma of that demonic nightmare, one week later I had an even more foreboding encounter with the powers of darkness.

On May 2, 2001, in the wee hours of the morning (2:35 AM, to be exact), I was awakened by the involuntary, uncontrollable trembling of my arms and hands. While trying to collect my thoughts, a wave of trembling passed through my arms and hands again. And at that very moment, I was struck with a strong sense of fear. But there was something peculiar about this fear. It wasn't fear as an emotion, but rather as a *presence*. The atmosphere of my bedroom was permeated with the raw presence of fear! I had never experienced anything like it. And during those few fleeting seconds, while trying to make sense of what was happening to me, the Spirit of God spoke these exact words to my heart: *"The devil...it's the devil."* Laying on my stomach at the time, I quickly turned my head and peered over my right shoulder towards the middle of my bedroom. And to the right of the bedroom door I saw a dark, vapor-like presence swirling counter-clockwise in mid-air, becoming thicker and darker by the moment, as if beginning to materialize into bodily form. (I'm sure the Holy Spirit wanted me to use my spiritual authority in this situation, but a great sense of dread had already swept over my entire being, so much so that I could not even *think* about rebuking the devil in Jesus's name, let alone actually doing it.) The first and only thought that came to my mind was, *"Run!"*

One of my colleagues in ministry had been staying with me at the time, so I darted out of the master bedroom and crashed into the guest room where he was sound asleep. With hot tears streaming down my face, I slapped the light switch on and shouted, *"Frantz, wake up…wake up! The devil's in my bedroom!"* No sooner than I had spoken those words out of my mouth, that same horrific presence rushed in behind me and, in a matter of seconds, filled the entire guest room. Overwhelmed with sheer fright, we sat there completely immobilized, unable to utter a word. The very thought that Satan was standing in the room with us, having come in person himself to oppose me, was more than a little traumatizing. Moreover, the indescribably macabre presence that accompanied that diabolic visitation was in and of itself alone emotionally incapacitating. However, as we sat there quaking for dear life, the devil quite suddenly departed, and in the wake of his departure there immediately came a heavenly fragrance. An extraordinarily sweet aroma with hints of lilac suddenly filled the entire room. It was a smell unlike anything on earth. I then knew it was the "odor of paradise," that sacred fragrance I had heard and read so much about from the testimonials of others. The apostle, Paul, and a few of his colleagues had been privileged by God to have this divine odor accompany them wherever they traveled to preach and teach the Word of God. As it is written,

Now thanks be unto God, which always causeth us to triumph in Christ, and maketh manifest the savour of His knowledge by us in every place. For we are unto God a sweet savour of Christ…

2 Corinthians 2:14, 15

This wondrous, floral-like scent was a sign, a portent that God had sent one of His valiant angels to drive the devil away from us. Needless to say, my colleague and I, overjoyed by the immediate intervention of the Lord, lifted our hands and poured out praises of thanksgiving to the Father for protecting us during that spine-tingling confrontation with the prince of the power of the air.

Even so, after finding the courage to return to my bedroom, I kept all the lights on when I went back to sleep, still enervated by that visitation from Satan. To think that out of 6.5 billion people on earth, the one whom ancient Scripture calls **"the god of this world"** (2 Cor. 4:3, 4) personally came to terrorize *me*, of all people. It is one thing to read about the devil on paper. Yet, quite another thing for that same devil to come and oppose you in person! I can now empathize with Joshua, the Lord's high priest, who once saw,

> **...Satan standing at his right hand to resist him.**
>
> Zechariah 3:1

What did I do? What did I stumble upon that was so threatening that the chief *persona non grata* himself came in person to oppose me? The Spirit of the Lord revealed that it was my public disclosure about the existence of the angel of prosperity just two weeks prior, and of my God-given authority to invoke that angel at will, that caused such a stir within the demonic ranks, the reverberation of which reached into the upper echelon of the kingdom of darkness and eventually into the ears of Satan himself!

Prosperity! All I did that Sunday afternoon was to talk publicly about an angel of prosperity. What is it about prosperity that provokes the devil to such fury? For years I had engaged in healing the sick, teaching Scripture, exorcising demons, prophesying oracles, evangelizing the lost, and debating Bible doctrine with cult leaders. Yet, in all those years I had never received such immediate and colossal backlash from the kingdom of darkness as I did when once I revealed my God-ordained alliance with the holy angel of prosperity.

Savior From Poverty

Indeed, the gates of Hell shall not prevail against the Prosperity Movement, for as the venerable rabbi, Gamaliel, said so succinctly,

If it be of God, ye cannot overthrow it; lest haply ye be found even to fight against God.

Acts 5:39

So important is your prosperity to the heart of the Father that He did all in His power to guarantee that you prosper in life. This He did by sending His precious Son to die in abject poverty as your substitute so that, through His vicarious sacrifice, you could be rich! As inscribed in the sacred epistles,

For ye know the grace of our Lord Jesus Christ, that, though He was rich, yet for your sakes He became poor, that ye through His poverty might be rich.

2 Corinthians 8:9

For many years now, Jesus Christ has been typecast in movies, books, magazines, and pulpits as a poor itinerant preacher who, with a small band of uneducated men, wandered about from place to place telling colorful stories about God and the importance of good deeds while living off the handouts of charitable people. Yet, truth be told, Scripture says otherwise. Jesus actually was a rich prophet from Nazareth who was highly respected by the rich (Lk. 19:1-6), whose ministry was financially underwritten by the rich (Mk. 12:41; Lk. 8:1-3), and who, when He died, was buried among the rich by the rich (Isa. 53:9; Matt. 27:57-60). Everything about

Jesus's life smacked of affluence, even to the point where He chose only to ride upon a donkey **"whereon man never sat"** (Mk. 11:1-6 c.f. Ps. 45:3, 4). Moreover, He wore only those bodily fragrances which were found, not in the marketplaces of the common people, but among those fine quality parfums accessible only to the wealthy within the palaces of the elite (Ps. 45:8). He also had a personal accountant whom He would customarily require to take portions of His immense wealth with which to donate to charity (Jn. 13:29). In fact, Christ was so financially prosperous that, when He was crucified, a band of Roman soldiers standing at the foot of the cross, perceiving the elegance of His clothing, actually gambled among themselves to determine who would get to keep His crème de la crème coat, a tailor-made coat that was seamless from top to bottom (Jn. 19:23, 24)!

In the mind of the Father, the plundering of Jesus's material wealth at Calvary, because it was vicarious in nature, was credited to your account! This He did so that, once becoming born again, you could experience material abundance throughout the remainder of your life.

That is why it is imperative for you to understand the significant role the prophet is to play in your life for, indeed, as a prophet of God I am a stockbroker of the Kingdom of Heaven. And it is my responsibility and privilege to use my divine gifting to help you manifest your prosperity. As it is written,

Believe His prophets, so shall ye prosper.

2 Chronicles 20:20

My particular gifting--by the will of God--is to invoke the angel of prosperity into the lives of all those who simply ask. And he whose name is secret will ratify this sacred "Covenant of Prosperity" which Jesus Christ as its Supreme Benefactor, sealed with His own blood in the valley of Golgotha.

Your heavenly Father--because He loves you--directed this book into your hands so that, upon receiving your request, I could invoke the prosperity angel to come to your house to bless you. And that precise moment will signify the beginning of a glorious era of prosperity miracles in your life, for indeed,

The Lord, before whom I walk, will send His angel with thee, and prosper thy way.

Genesis 24:40

Cases In Point

One Monday afternoon I invoked the angel of prosperity to bless a man named Earl. And three days later he was given an unexpected check for $900! He was so overjoyed that the following Tuesday he asked me to invoke the angel of prosperity to bless him again. I did, and the very next day someone else unexpectedly gave him $500!

I invoked the angel of prosperity to bless Carmen with a court case involving an automobile accident. Shortly thereafter the judge threw the case out! After which time she soon landed the best paying job of her life! A practical stranger even paid for her to go to school for her real estate license! Moreover, she was happily married within that same year!

I invoked the angel of prosperity to bless Toni who, at the time, was renting a room in someone else's home. Some time later she moved into her own apartment and was for the first time approved for two major credit cards after having been repeatedly turned down!

I invoked the angel of prosperity to bless Theresa. And within two weeks she was working at another job with better pay and better benefits, in closer proximity to her place of residence than her previous job!

I invoked the angel of prosperity to bless Jennifer. And within thirty days a $15,000 hospital bill which she incurred through surgery (the amount of which became the source of much stress and anxiety) was completely liquidated, compliments of the hospital itself!

I invoked the angel of prosperity to bless Steven, an auto mechanic. And within a week and a half he received the best paying job of his life, making $250 more per week than his previous job, doing the same exact work!

I invoked the angel of prosperity to bless Elisabeth. And in two days she found $8,500 in a brief case, in a ghetto project of all places! Moreover, within another three weeks she obtained the best paying job of her life!

I invoked the angel of prosperity to bless Mitch, a truck driver who lamented that he could not find any work. And within two months he had so much work coming in that he literally had to turn away offers!

I invoked the angel of prosperity to bless Tamara. And in a matter of a few months she went from renting a room in a poverty-stricken home to living in a luxury apartment home in an upscale community, with a new and better job with better pay, and with a brand new car!

I invoked the angel of prosperity to bless Kema, who was about to close down her hair salon because of a lack of clientele. And within a week and a half she began having such an influx of business that she and her staff literally had to begin locking the door to the salon and turning customers away!

I invoked the angel of prosperity to bless Ingrid, who had been unemployed for a considerable amount of time. And the very next day a complete stranger (for no apparent reason) gave her $60. Moreover, she was gainfully employed within three weeks time!

I invoked the angel of prosperity to bless Esther, who had no automobile at the time. And within a month (in spite of bad credit and only a part-time job) she drove off the lot with a brand new car, no money down, and obtained a full-time job doing the kind of work she loved doing!

I invoked the angel of prosperity to bless Diane, a semi-literate woman who lived in ghetto-like conditions her entire life. And within a matter of months, by a series of unmistakable miracles, she was living in a nice new residence in an upscale community, and even drove off a car lot in a brand new car--the best she'd ever had--with a check for $63, compliments of the car dealer!

I invoked the angel of prosperity to bless Dwynnifer. And the very next day, before stepping out of the front door to go to work, she was contacted by a family member who informed her that she was going to give her a house!

I invoked the angel of prosperity to bless Ondrea. And within a matter of days $1,100 was mysteriously deleted from two delinquent car notes, car notes which the car dealer could absolutely find no record of!

I invoked the angel of prosperity to bless Ashley, a 15 year old employee of a fast food restaurant who was told (due to management error) she would not be getting her paycheck until after the Christmas holiday. The very next day, an elderly customer sitting off to the side overheard her relating the matter to a fellow employee. Seeing the girl's despondency he was moved with compassion and gave her $100 cash! Moreover, the very next day the store manager--although on vacation--decided to come to the store and draft her a paycheck after all!

I invoked the angel of prosperity to bless Bessie whose hair salon business was three months behind in rent. And the very next day while speaking with the landlord via telephone, he decided to excuse all three months of the back rent! Moreover, a few days later she was contacted by the city hall of a town where she owned a small piece of property. They told her she had overpaid on her property taxes (which she insists she did not) and that they would be promptly returning to her over $2,300!

These few cases in point (and many others too numerous to mention in this brief writing) attest to the fact that there truly exists an *angel of prosperity*. And the moment I step into the intersection between time and eternity (cloaked with the prophetic mantle) and call out to the heavens on your behalf, that very same prosperity angel will come to you riding upon the wings of the wind--*and bless you!* Thus it is to your supreme benefit to allow me the distinct privilege of praying for you. As the Lord Himself vouchsafed,

For he is a prophet, and he shall pray for thee.

Genesis 20:7

Two Paths To Riches

Some time ago noted economist and author Paul Zane Pilzer, wrote a bestselling book entitled, *God Wants You To Be Rich*. To the discerning mind, the only thing more beautiful than the title of that book is that most excellent verse of holy scripture supporting its claim, which says,

The blessing of the Lord, it maketh rich, and He addeth no sorrow with it.

Proverbs 10:22

Yes! *God wants you to be rich!* It is your Christian birthright to be rich (Rom. 8:16, 17)! And your heavenly Father wants you to be rich so that you--regal child of God that you are--can be beautifully and lavishly clothed, housed, furnished, transported and supplied with all the fabulous things this world has to offer. This is precisely what the Lord was talking about when He promised you,

And I will give thee the treasures of darkness, and hidden riches of secret places, that thou mayest know that I, the Lord, which call thee by thy name, am the God of Israel.

Isaiah 45:3

Your heavenly Father wants to pamper you with *"the treasures of darkness"* and *"hidden riches of secret places,"* meaning unique, one of a kind, hard to locate luxuries, because He loves you.

The Word of God goes on to say,

Labour not to be rich: cease from thine own wisdom.

Proverbs 23:4

Why would the Bible announce that God wants you to be rich, then turn around and caution you about laboring to be rich? Is this a contradiction in terms? By no means, for Jehovah is simply cautioning you about traveling down the wrong path to riches.

Actually, there are two basic paths that lead to riches: the path of one's own wisdom and the path of the Lord's favor. When a person strives to be rich by his own wisdom and ability he often pays a heavy price in the process, e. g., the breakdown of health or family relations, engaging in illegal activities which eventually lead to imprisonment, or some other kind of unnecessary travesty. Moreover, the wealth that comes about in this manner oftentimes is a fleeting wealth that does not last. That is why the Holy Manuscript admonishes us,

Wealth gotten by vanity shall be diminished.

Proverbs 13:11

And again,

...the prosperity of fools shall destroy them.

Proverbs 1:32

However, when a person positions himself to become rich through the power of God's favor, no type of sorrow or disappointment whatsoever comes with those riches but only peace, happiness, and a well deserved sense of contentment. This is the very thing Jedidiah had in mind when he wrote,

Every man also to whom God hath given riches and wealth, and hath given him power to eat thereof, and to take his portion, and to rejoice in his labour; this is the gift of God.

Ecclesiastes 5:19

68 / When The Angel of Prosperity Comes To Your House

Your Father which is in Heaven (in response to my prayer for you) is about to charge His mighty angel of prosperity to come and pour out upon you the splendor of His favor, which favor, incidentally, is a type of perennial grace--an inexplicable charisma, if you would--that will cause you to prosper beyond your fondest dreams. As the son of Sirach proclaimed,

> **His favour bringeth prosperity forever.**
>
> Ecclesiasticus 11:17

Yes! Almighty God is about to bless you with riches and wealth-- and give you the ability to enjoy it all! This is His gift to you. And if you will travel this path of divine favor for the rest of your life--a path that leads to true and lasting riches--when the time draws nigh for you to go home and see the Lord in peace, your epitaph, like King David's, will read that you,

> **...died in a good old age, full of days, riches, and honour.**
>
> 1 Chronicles 29:28

He Blessed Him There

No matter what you may be going through at this very moment in your life, it is time for you to lift your hands and your voice and shout for joy because you know that *you have a divine right to be rich!* And he whose name remains secret has the power to bless you so that you can become rich! For the Scripture reveals,

And Jacob asked him, and said, Tell me, I pray thee, thy name. And he said, Wherefore is it that thou dost ask after my name? And he blessed him there.

Genesis 32:29

Notice the prosperity angel (whose name remains secret) blessed Jacob "there," Not somewhere other than where Jacob was at the time, but *there,* right where he was at that moment. And what the angel of prosperity did for Jacob (and many others) he can and will do for *you.*

Each day multitudes of people can be found traveling the world over, visiting shrines, temples, monasteries, ashrams, grottos, pagodas, and other holy places so called, seeking a particular blessing. But there is no need for any of that. As Emerson was so bold to say, *"Traveling is a fool's paradise. The wise man stays at home."* Why travel anywhere to receive the Lord's blessing when His holy angel of prosperity is perched on the edge of Paradise, ready and willing to swoop down and bless you *there,* right where you are?

> Awake,
>
> O herald of deity;
>
> Unfurl
>
> Your grace-tipped wings...
>
> And come down.
>
> Swoop,
>
> Thou intrepid visitor,
>
> With sacred vial in hand, and
>
> Prosper

When The Angel of Prosperity Comes To Your House

The offspring of God!

Pour out of the abundance of the

Bounty

Of the Almighty, and let

Prosperity miracles flow;

Flow

Like a babbling brook of

Bountiful blessings

Beyond the boundaries of a

Luscious new life.

So shall we

Dance

With reckless abandon as we

Drink

Everlastingly from the

Cornucopia

Of the Lord!

Believe the prophet when I tell you that, when the angel of prosperity comes to your house to bless you, that day will mark a major shift in the course and direction of your life, ushering you into a state of such financial and material abundance that all your acquaintances will be compelled to confess that your life, and everything about it, consists of the stuff legends are made of!

The Moment of Truth

Finally, child of God, the moment of truth has arrived when revelation must gracefully bow out so that application may come and do what it does best--*make things happen.* So, if the Spirit of the Lord has quickened the revelation of this book to your heart and you desire prayer for the angel of prosperity to come and bless you, simply write to me so I can rush you a vial of my *angel oil.* Yes, angels are powerful, but they also have limitations. Unlike God, they are not all knowing. That is why the children of Israel, during their sojourn in the land of Egypt, had to anoint the doorposts of their homes with lamb's blood so that the angel of judgment would know which houses to pass over (Ex. 12:21-30).

Consequently, without this oil, the angel of prosperity will have difficulty finding your house. But once you anoint the doorposts of your house with this sacred oil, the Lord's prosperity angel will at once be able to locate your residence, and come to your house and bless you! So hurry and write to me today so I can rush you my blessed *angel oil,* a combination of oil essences mixed by divine revelation, then sealed with an ancient prayer.

I'll be waiting to hear from you. And until I do, I leave you with this gentle reminder:

> **The eternal God is thy refuge, and underneath are the everlasting arms.**
>
> Deuteronomy 33:27

Amen.

Prayer for Salvation

Jesus Christ,

I understand that my life is a gift from God, the Creator of the universe. And in appreciation for that gift, it is both my privilege and my moral responsibility to live my life in a way that is pleasing to Him. As the Bible says,

Let us hear the conclusion of the whole matter: Fear God, and keep His commandments: for this is the whole duty of man.

Ecclesiastes 12:13

I also understand that, because of the sin of the first human being, Adam (Gen. 3:1-24), I was born in sin (Ps. 51:5), having inherited a nature that compels me to do things contrary to the will of God (Rom. 3:2, 5:15-19). Consequently, I have no ability, in my own strength, to properly bring God the glory He deserves, and that the ultimate penalty for living my life contrary to God's will is eternal damnation (Rev. 20:15).

Jesus, I understand that you--an innocent, sinless man--were chosen by God to die on a cross as the Substitute for my sins so that, having accepted by faith what you did for me on the cross, I would be delivered from the effects of hereditary sin and be saved from eternal damnation. I understand, Lord Jesus, that salvation is a free gift (Rom. 6:33) given to all those who believe in the truth of your vicarious death and resurrection (2 Cor. 5:21), and who simply ask you to be the Lord of their lives. As the Bible says,

That if thou shalt confess with thy mouth the Lord Jesus, and shalt believe in thine heart that God hath raised Him from the dead, thou shalt be saved. For with the heart man believeth unto unrighteousness; and with the mouth confession is made unto salvation...For whosoever shall call upon the Name of the Lord shall be saved.

Romans 10:9, 10, 13

Jesus, I believe in my heart that God raised you from the dead, and I now ask you to become my personal Lord and Savior from this day forward. Thank you for hearing and answering my prayer. According to your Word, the Bible, I am now saved. I am now born again. I am now a child of God. Amen.

Signed_____

Date_____

If you just prayed this prayer for the first time to receive Jesus Christ as your Lord and Savior, please take a moment and write to us at *The Prophetic Society* and tell us your testimony. We want to send you some materials that will aid you in developing your newfound relationship with the Lord. God bless you!

Printed in Great Britain
by Amazon